The Perils of Isabella the Great Dane

Rio

DEPARTURE

NY

HOLLYWOOD

ARRIVAL

Miami

PASSPO

MIGRATION

By **Mel Gorham**

A True Story / Una Historia Verdadera

SERVICE DOG

THIS BOOK IS DEDICATED TO:
ISABELLA
"THE GREATEST DAME OF THEM ALL"
June 8, 2009- February 5, 2020

Mel Gorham is a work in progress. Mel has been called a true force of nature. She was born Marilyn Schnier from a Cuban Catholic mother and an American Jewish father. An only child (who never had children) a true eccentric New Yorker, who loves Great Danes.

The first children's book ever read to her by her Jewish grandmother Minnie was "Suzuki Beane" which totally inspired Mel to write "The Perils of Isabella the Great Dane."

Mel has been a successful actress in many Hollywood films, had her own tv sitcom on NBC, & was in several Broadway Plays & musicals in NYC...and now decided to write a book for children about the treatment of animals on planet Earth.

Mel is also a professional artist & documentary film maker, and now, a first time author.

This book is a true story told by her favorite Great Dane, Isabella.

Enjoy!

Photo credit: Johanna Siegmann

Photo credit: Jerry Hinkle shootfashion.com

Archway Publishing books may be ordered through booksellers or by contacting:

Archway Publishing
1663 Liberty Drive
Bloomington, IN 47403
www.archwaypublishing.com
1 (888) 242-5904

Because of the dynamic nature of the Internet, any web addresses or links contained in this book may have changed since publication and may no longer be valid. The views expressed in this work are solely those of the author and do not necessarily reflect the views of the publisher, and the publisher hereby disclaims any responsibility for them.

Any people depicted in stock imagery provided by Getty Images are models, and such images are being used for illustrative purposes only.
Certain stock imagery © Getty Images.

ISBN: 978-1-4808-8845-6 (sc)
ISBN: 978-1-4808-8844-9 (hc)
ISBN: 978-1-4808-8843-2 (e)

Print information available on the last page.

Archway Publishing rev. date: 02/21/2020

Dedicated To:

My Grandmaw Emma

(1935-2004)

This is Mac...He is My Father.

Este es Mac...el es Mi Papa.

He was the first Cuban...to escape Cuba in 1962 on a kayak.
El salio de Cuba en 1962 rumbo a una nueva vida en USA
remando en su kayak.

He is a real hero...and a successful businessman.
El es un héroe...y ahora un triunfante hombre
de negocios en USA.

And almost retired at 76.
Y todavía trabaja a pesar de tener 76 años.

This is Mel...who loves dogs and all animals.
Esta es Mel...ella ama los perros y todos los animales.

She is a really cool lady...and is a Vegan too!
Ella es una dama muy moderna...¡ella es vegetariana!

She's My Mother.
Ella es Mi Mama.

She was a successful actress

in the movies...

on Broadway...

and

on T.V.

Mi Mama fue una artista muy famosa

en las películas...

en Broadway...

y

la Televisión.

She has anxiety and needs tender loving care around her at all times...And I am her "Special Dog" who helps her a lot.

Ella padece de ansiedad...yo soy quien la acompaña y la ayuda siempre en esos momentos.

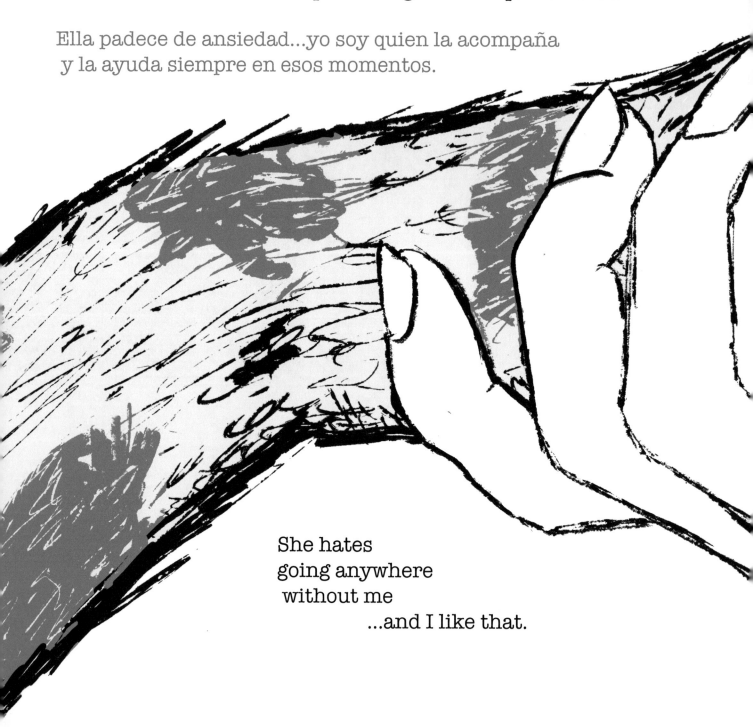

She hates
going anywhere
 without me
          ...and I like that.

Ella detesta estar
sin mi compañia

...y a mi me
gusta que
asi sea.

Collins Ave
A1A ➡

We have a great time here, and we throw a lot of parties.
Nosotros nos divertimos mucho aquí, y tenemos muchas fiestas

I am part of the human family, so I am invited to every party and family gathering.

Yo soy otro miembro de la familia humana, y estoy invitada a todas las fiestas y reuniones familiares.

People love petting me because I am so unusually tall and long-legged.

A las personas les encanta acariciarme, tal vez porque soy un perro grande de patas largas.

And I often go to my Grandpaw's assisted living facility...to make the older people there happy!

Mi Mama me lleva a visitar a mi "Abuelo", el vive en una casa de asistencia para personas mayores... ellos se alegran y divierten mucho cuando yo los visito.

They pet me and I like to
play with them!

Ellos me acarician y a mi
me encanta jugar con ellos!

I was born in Brazil...

and that is where Mel found me,

when I was only 3 months old.

Yo naci en Brazil...

donde Mama Mel me encontró

cuando yo tenia solos

tres meses

de nacida.

She saved my life because no one wanted me.

I was the runt of the litter,

and my color

wasn't a popular color for Great Dane buyers.

Mi Mama me salvo la vida porque nadie me quería,

todos mis hermanos eran mas lindos que yo.

Mi color no es el preferido por las personas que tienen

perros Gran Daneses.

The minute Mel and I met,
we fell madly in love.

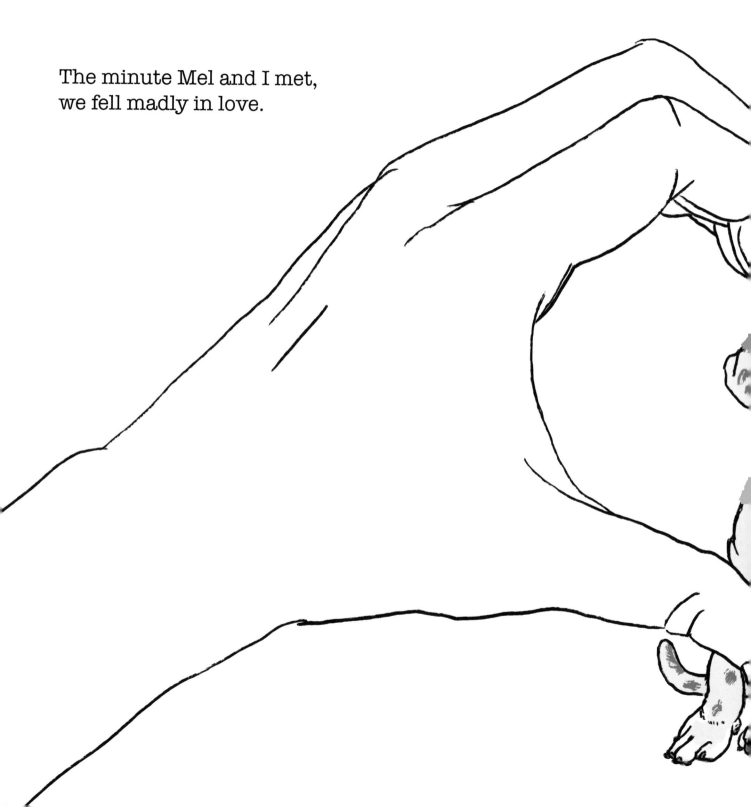

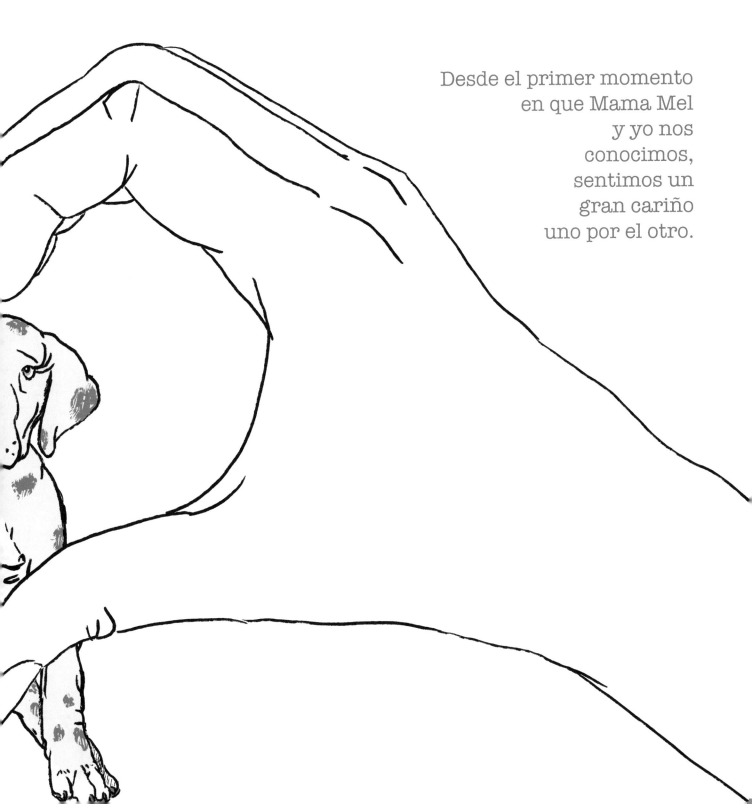

Desde el primer momento
en que Mama Mel
y yo nos
conocimos,
sentimos un
gran cariño
uno por el otro.

She then took me in a cargo box below
the airplane to New York City...

Mama Mel me llevo con ella en un
avion para la ciudad de Nueva York,
pero yo tuve que viajar en una
pequeña caja para perros
junto con las maletas
de las personas...

...Where we lived for a few years
before we met Mac.

...Donde vivimos por unos años
antes de conocer a Mac.

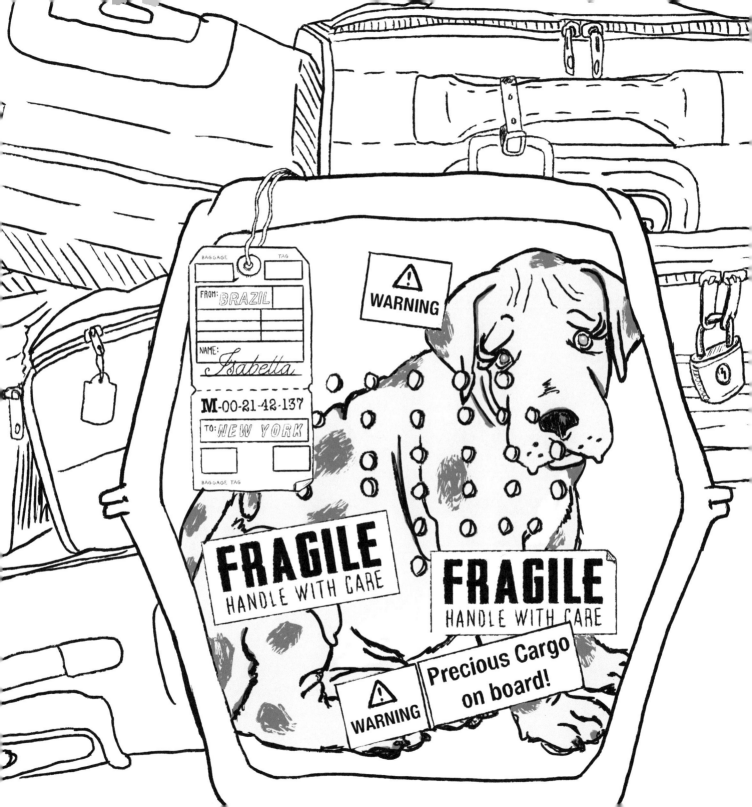

I used to sleep right next to her...

Yo usualmente dormia en la cama con Mi Mama...

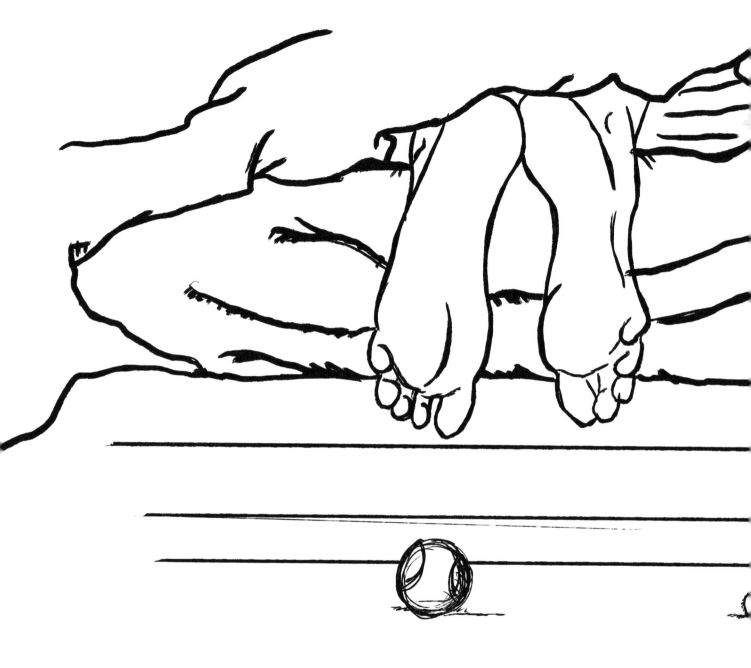

...until Mac came along.

...hasta que llego Mac.

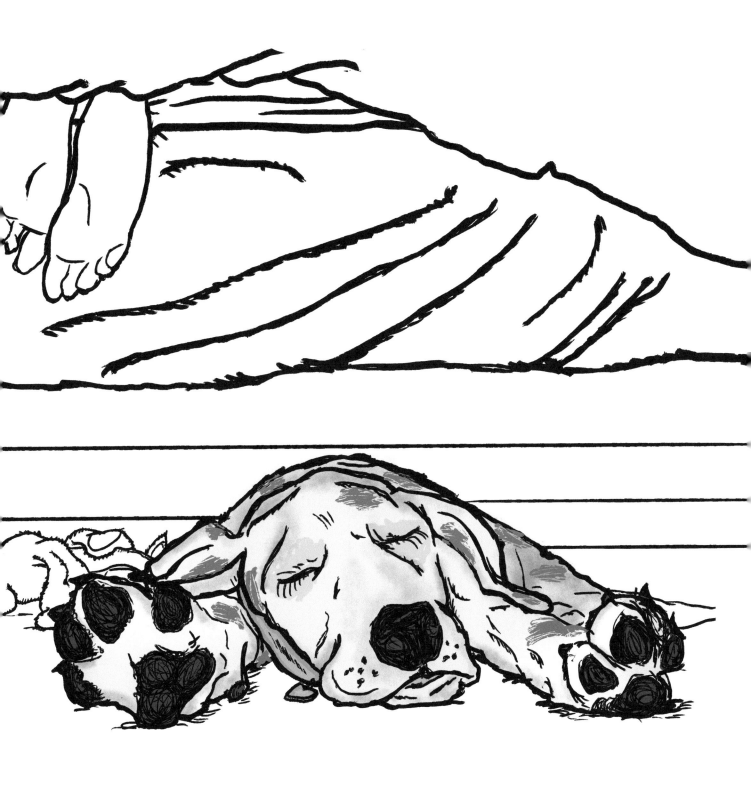

Mel also took me, for a while, to live in Los Angeles, California where all the movie stars live!

¡Mama Mel tambien me llevo a vivir con ella a Los Angeles, California, donde viven todas las estrellas del cine!

I loved driving with Mel...
She took me everywhere!

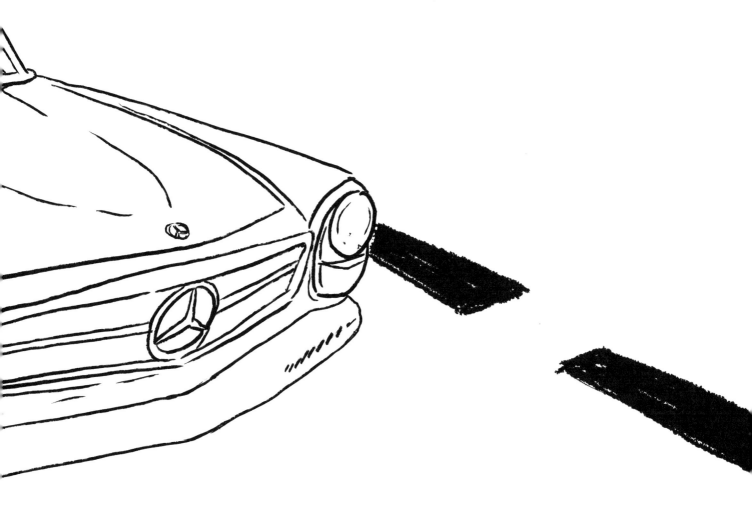

Me encantaba salir a pasear con Mama Mel...
¡Ella me llevava a todos los lugares!

When I lived in New York with my cool Mom Mel,
she often took me to Madison Square Dog Park,
where I was the Queen of the dog world.

Cuando yo vivia en Nueva York con Mama Mel,
ella me llevaba con frequencia a el parque Madison
Square Dog Park, donde yo era la Reina entre
todos los perros en el parque.

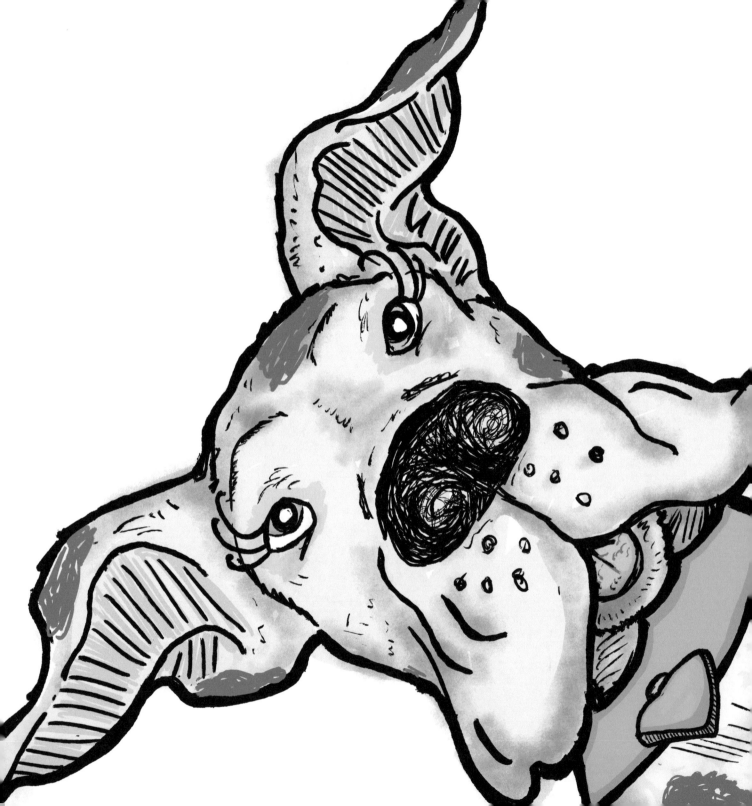

Because
I was
the
biggest
breed
there,
until
one day

...when I met Dana the Great Dane.

De todos
los perros
en el parque
yo
era
la mas
grande,
hasta
que
un dia

...conoci a Dana la Gran Danesa.

She became my best friend until Mel
decided to move to Miami Beach.

Dana fue mi mejor amiga hasta que Mama
Mel decidio mudarse a Miami Beach.

When it snowed in Manhattan, my Mom would put a big sweater on me with a matching scarf and we would walk everywhere together and people would always pull their cameras out and take pictures of us...We were famous!

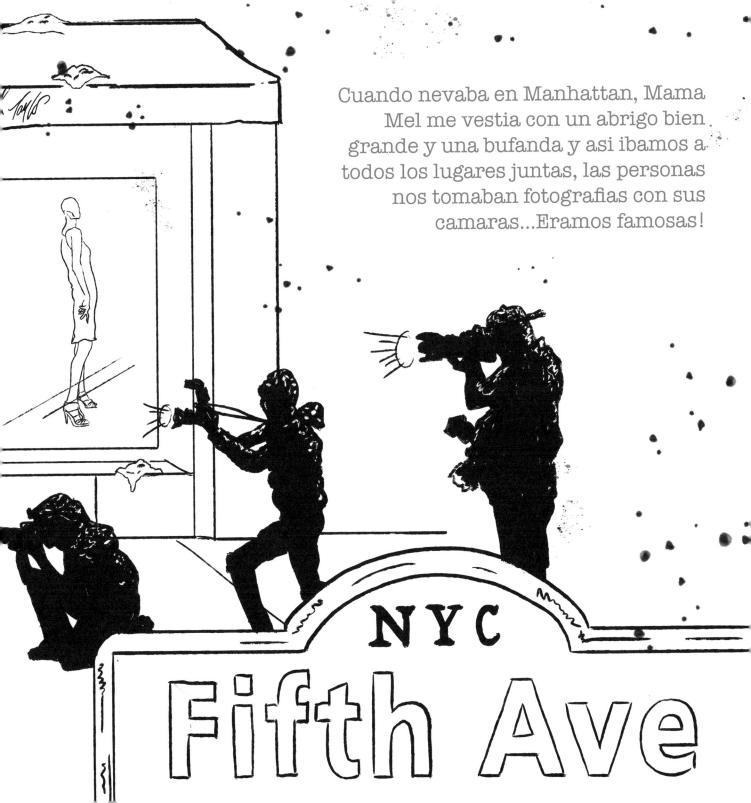

Cuando nevaba en Manhattan, Mama Mel me vestia con un abrigo bien grande y una bufanda y asi ibamos a todos los lugares juntas, las personas nos tomaban fotografias con sus camaras...Eramos famosas!

NYC

Fifth Ave

One day my well-known Mom woke up and decided to quit acting and pursue bigger and better things. So she wrote a letter of resignation to the entertainment world.

Dear Hollywood,
It was fun while it lasted.
But it's time that I move on
to bigger and better things....

I watched her in awe and she explained to me that we were moving to Miami Beach so that we could be with my Grandpaw Sanford because he was getting old and we were all he had.

Un dia mi Mama decidio no actuar mas en las peliculas, y escribio una carta informando a todo el mundo sus intenciones. Me explico que nos íbamos a vivir a Miami Beach para asi poder estar mas cerca de abuelo Sanford porque el no tenia mas familia que nosotros.

So there we were, just arrived on Miami Beach. We had no furniture because it was all coming on a big truck from Manhattan. So we slept together on the floor for days on a bunch of blankets.

Asi que ahi estabamos en Miami Beach, no teniamos muebles porque ellos llegaban en un camión desde Manhattan. Dormimos en el piso juntas con muchas frazadas.

Even though it was really hot out, we would take long walks
on Miami Beach together. She had my leash in
one hand and a glass of Champagne in the other.
Such a character my Mom is!

Aunque hacia mucho calor, mi mama y yo saliamos a caminar
en la playa, ella llevaba mi collar en una mano
y una copa de Champaña en la otra mano.
¡Mi Mama tiene un carácter muy comico!

Then one day, along came Mr. Good Looking...Mel was set up on a blind date and she went on it and left me with her friend and her old dog, a Boxer with an attitude. For a while we were really good friends, until she got uppity and viciously attacked me out of jealousy. We both ended up in the hospital.

Todo iba bien hasta que un dia apareció Mac que era guapo... Mel y Mac salieron de paseo una tarde y me dejaron con su amiga quien tenia un perro Boxer con mala actitud. Por un tiempo nos llevamos bien hasta que un dia ella estaba celosa de la atención que yo recibia y me ataco. Las dos terminamos en el hospital.

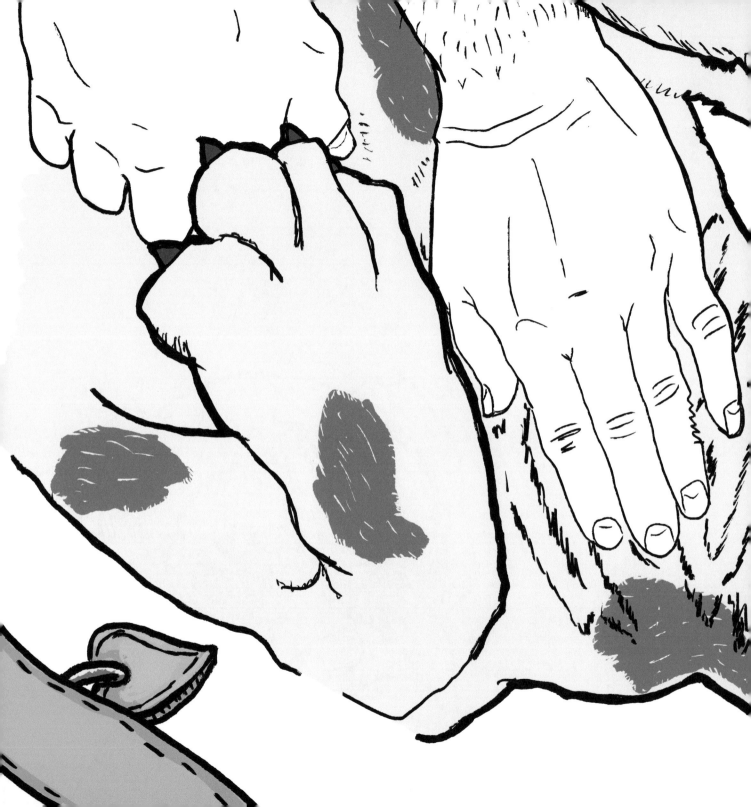

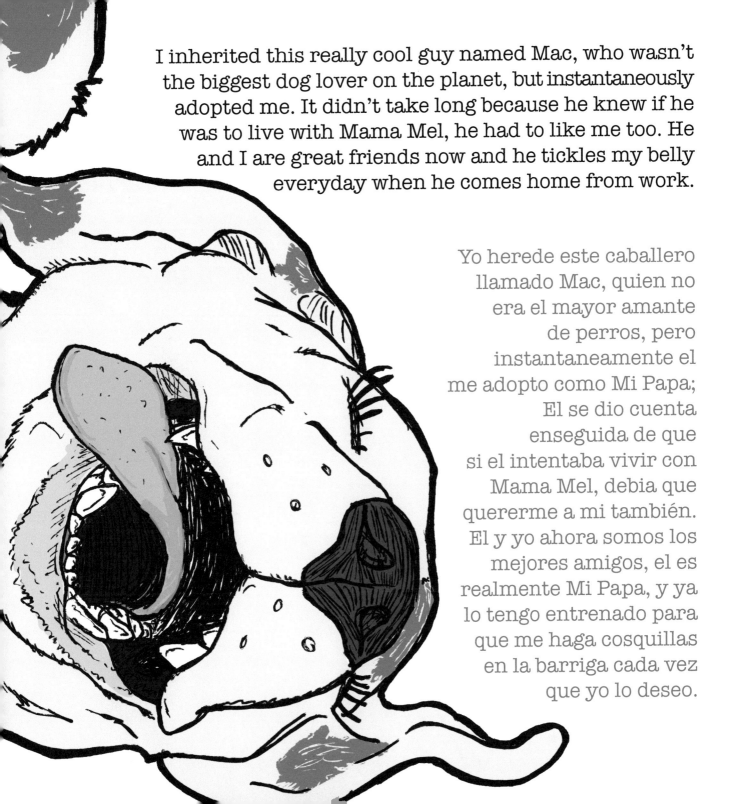

I inherited this really cool guy named Mac, who wasn't the biggest dog lover on the planet, but instantaneously adopted me. It didn't take long because he knew if he was to live with Mama Mel, he had to like me too. He and I are great friends now and he tickles my belly everyday when he comes home from work.

Yo herede este caballero llamado Mac, quien no era el mayor amante de perros, pero instantaneamente el me adopto como Mi Papa; El se dio cuenta enseguida de que si el intentaba vivir con Mama Mel, debia que quererme a mi también. El y yo ahora somos los mejores amigos, el es realmente Mi Papa, y ya lo tengo entrenado para que me haga cosquillas en la barriga cada vez que yo lo deseo.

At first, and for a very long time,
I was not allowed on the bed at all.

Por mucho tiempo, no me permitian que yo subiera
a la cama con ellos.

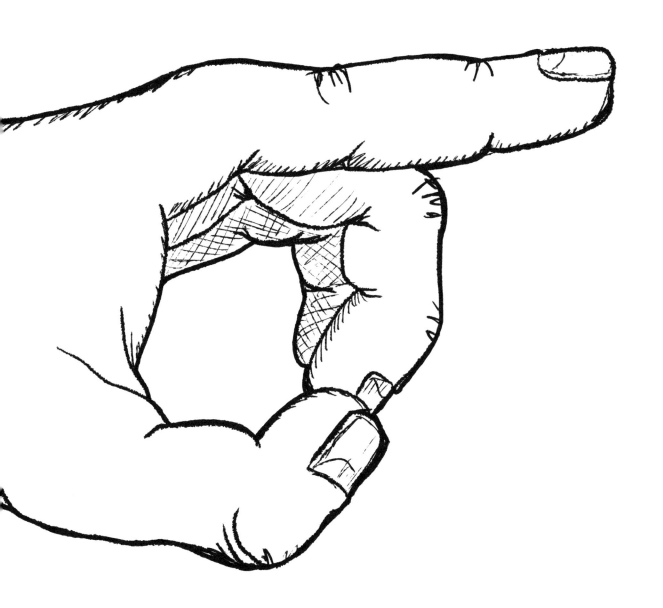

Now that I am getting old, I spend a lot of time sleeping in Mac & Mel's bed, which has become partially mine.

Ahora que yo he envejecido, paso mucho tiempo con Mac y Mel en su cama, que ahora es mia también.

There are some people in my building that really like me, but then there are some people who hate dogs in general...and dislike me because of my size and are always looking to find something wrong with me living there.

Hay muchas personas en el edificio donde yo vivo que realmente me quieren, pero hay otras que no le gustan los perros en general, incluyendome a mi, no les gusto por mi tamaño y siempre buscan motivos para que yo no pueda vivir ahí.

NO DOG ALLOWE

PLE CU YOUR

What these animal haters don't realize is that, while they are mistreating animals here on Earth, someday they are going to be held accountable for their actions. Animals are good and unconditional with their love to humans...

...SO, WHY DON'T WE GET THE SAME TREATMENT AND RESPECT IN RETURN!

No Admittance

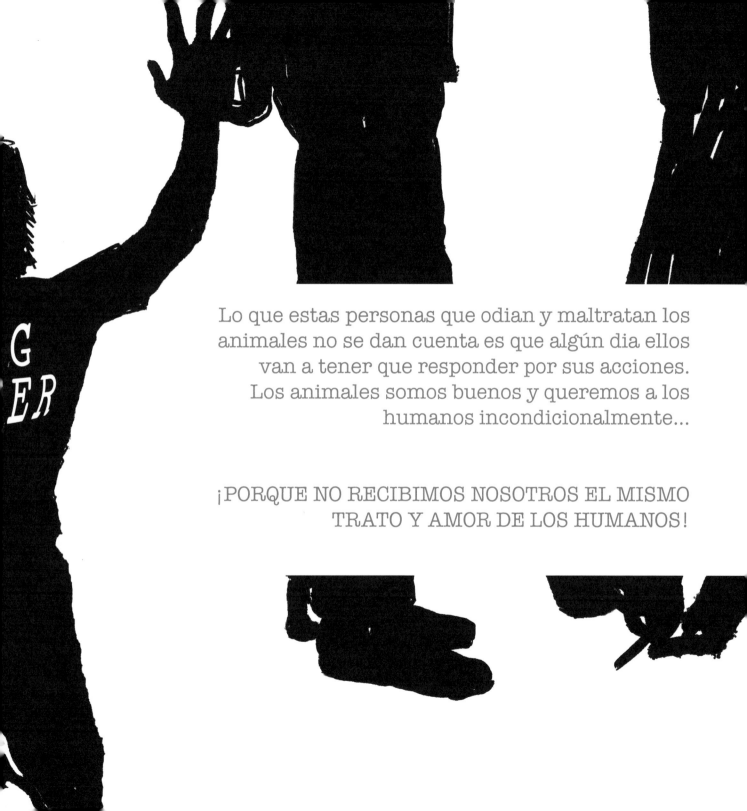

Lo que estas personas que odian y maltratan los animales no se dan cuenta es que algún dia ellos van a tener que responder por sus acciones. Los animales somos buenos y queremos a los humanos incondicionalmente...

¡PORQUE NO RECIBIMOS NOSOTROS EL MISMO TRATO Y AMOR DE LOS HUMANOS!

All we require is a little love, not much really. We are placed here on Earth just like humans are, so we should have the same choice to roam freely and to teach unconditional love and kindness to the humans who don't know what that is. We never complain about anything and need very little to be happy.

No requerimos más que un poco de amor, fuimos puestos aqui en la tierra igual que los humanos, deberiamos tener el mismo derecho de libremente habitar la tierra. Nosotros no nos quejamos de nada y requerimos muy poco para ser felices.

My Mom says she loves
animals just as much as people,
and I can understand why.
She is going to heaven.

Mama Mel dice que ella
ama los animales tanto
como a los humanos,
ella un dia ira al paraíso.

Nowadays, because I am 10 years old and that is 100 years old in human life...I just love sleeping in on rainy days. And now that my cool Mom is retired, we spend a lot of time together and we wouldn't have it any other way.

Ahora que ya yo tengo 10 años que es 100
años para un humano...me encanta dormir
mucho en los días lluviosos, y ya que Mi
Mama esta retirada, siempre estamos juntas
lo cual nos gusta muchísimo.

I have the best life any dog could ever ask for
and I am extremely grateful for it.

Yo disfruto de la mejor vida que un perro puede tener,
y por eso estoy eternamente agradecida.

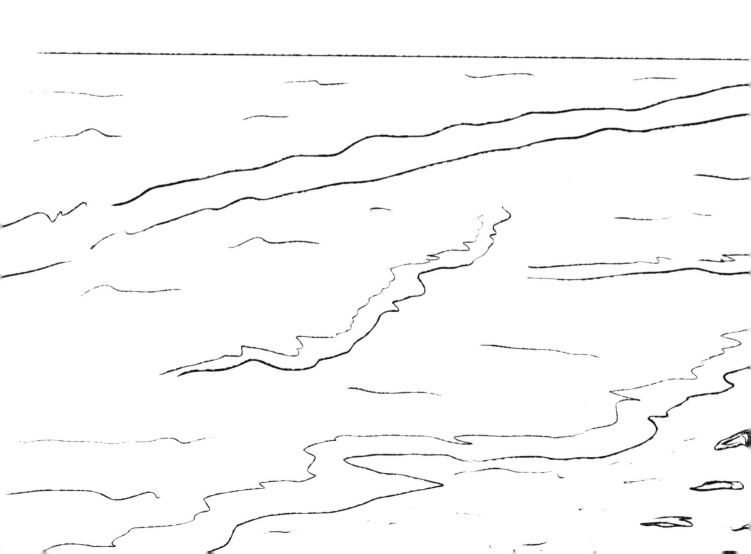

I am a very lucky dog!
¡Soy un perro muy dichoso!

"Until one has loved an animal, a part of one's soul remains unawakened." -Anatole France

"Hasta que uno no haya amado un animal, una parte de su alma permanece." -Anatole France

Nikolai Shorr is the Founder and Creative Director of Canal Street Counterfeit; a New York City - based design collective that specializes in creating commercial and fine art for a diverse client base. Nikolai's focus is on creating visual art that gets people *thinking, talking, smiling, laughing & challenging the status quo.* holler@ canalstreetcounterfeit.com

Printed in the United States
By Bookmasters